THE NOW DARK SKY, SETTING US ALL ON FIRE

CODHILL
PRESS

ALSO BY ROBERT KRUT

This Is the Ocean
The Spider Sermons

THE NOW DARK SKY, SETTING US ALL ON FIRE

POEMS

ROBERT KRUT

CODHILL PRESS

NEW YORK • NEW PALTZ

CODHILL
PRESS

Codhill books are published by
David Appelbaum for Codhill Press

codhill.com

THE NOW DARK SKY, SETTING US ALL ON FIRE

Published in the United States of America

ISBN 978-1-949933-03-1

Cover and Book Design by Jana Potashnik
BAIRDesign, Inc. • bairdesign.com

CONTENTS

Father I don't see our sunlit earth
The wolf swaddles it
With his black howl

It seems he pulls her
Out of her own root
Together with her golden
And his black and blue heart

—Vasko Popa, "Wolf's Earth"

1.

WELCOME

In the bulb of each fingertip,
the oval spheres of ten skulls—

in the lines on your hands,
a dirge melody waiting to echo—

in the reverse knuckles,
contorted demon face circled by fire.

And you would rather leave them all
behind while you walk away—

your ability to hold even the lightest
object, a lock of fine hair—

than hear that death song
every time you reach

to greet a stranger.

DIVINITY

Virus-blind, you stumble to an alley,
under a lentil rainstorm, a preacher
waves rudder arms to thunder,
makes lightning scatter until five canaries
escape his sleeves, singing condolences,
a misdirection from the transistor radio
around his neck, beneath his vestments,
its zealous torque fusing electrodes
to your breath, turning thoughts to words,
your face a cannon, and the realization
he was merely a collection of discarded
nightclub flyers lifted by the wind
between graffitied walls.

PHANTASMAGORIA AT SIX AM

In the alley between clubs, a guy shaves
in a stainless-steel plate hung to the wall.
With each sweep of the cream, his face
disappears until two eyes drift off, lost balloons.

The street is, of course, quiet.
A garbage truck glides by,
its hazards on, a cigarette lighting
the figure in the driver's seat.

In the only market open at this hour,
you buy water and day-old bread.
The guy behind the register is unimpressed
with the character trying to sell used lottery tickets.

The daylight peels silence
off the sides of buildings, revealing
the wide-open mouth of a graffiti face,
single vampire tooth, an arrow.

Nearby, a boombox props open a window,
a blast of music startles the pigeons
that burst to the sky, unveiling
a figure standing on the street, disoriented—

waves, tips a hat,
and you are gone.

YOU CAN'T ESCAPE WHEN YOU'VE BEEN UNDERWATER ALL ALONG

Fire the fingerprint police,
the sun-bleached searchers that turn
the righteous disks of inquiry,
those encompassing compasses, here
in the ocean caves where we breathe air,
sweet air, dewy with imprints of the shark
crimes, where waves carry long lost envelopes,
washed along with starfish that make forks
for the mighty, where above the prismed moon
is a tooth pushing through to eat us all,
God help us all, while we study a way to escape
when the whole time we've been nothing more
than animated bones in a chalice of blood
waiting to be swallowed whole.

THIS ALL STARTS WITH YOU, AND THIS ALL ENDS WITH YOU

A dragon sleeping on the roof, his tail trails the wall.

Your eyes invert themselves in sleep.

The stigmata were not from nails but snakes escaping.

A hook in the throat is a tooth in the heart.

The lawn of the world makes us all trespassers.

Please come call the clouds with me.

With a wind, see an ocean, with an ocean, see slate.

I'm ready for anything.

When my stomach is ripped from my body, I fully expect it.

Two horns were too much, and I now offer one to you.

A thousand leaves are worth one wish.

I forgot to forgo.

Crushing coal into diamond is crushing diamond into nothing.

I make myself a tree and I've been burying my feet for ages.

In the shoes of the world, the feet of the devil.

When the city turns its high rises inside out, the dimples will be your palm.

A helix firework explodes over the buildings.

THE VAULT

—woke up between a bracket
of buildings, looking into
their lobbies, the sliding doors
opening their mouths to marble,
the fluctuation of crowds
on their lunch break, costumes
prepare them for the stadium,
their secret handshakes, singing
confessions to the bank vaults
that house lockboxes, each full
of coins, strands of hair, and unsewn
buttons from the shirts of dead men.

NOW, BREATHE FIRE

Wait for the ash blanket and the concrete
wall of stone when the lights go out
and all you can breathe is smoke
until you adapt and cough up flames
in the night just in time to signal a getaway car
with no plates and everyone in town looks on—
but their eyes, dead comets in their skulls,
their teeth falling out as they call to you—
but you're already gone, gone to light
the fire that will turn this whole place
to scaffolding holding ashes, ashes, and
ashes again.

ONE ATTACKS THE OTHER

In an engineless car oceanside,
I sit taking notes and marking X's
in two columns on scrap paper.

Along the cliff ahead, a stranger pulls
petals off a mock orange shrub,
lets the wind lift them from his palm.

Empty envelope on the passenger seat,
I draw horizontal lines above the address,
let the saltwater air seal it for delivery.

And above, barreling inland,
two bats frightened by early daylight
attack a seagull, midair.

ATONAL BREATHING

Every molecule of air
communicates fear, each moth
circles the dead tree on the parkway
mourning its branches,
while we stand, trying
to breathe poison in this failing
kidney of the city,
the truck-sized foot of an invisible
giant hovering above us, knowing
that this, this simultaneous
inhale and exhale,
this shortcut to dread, this constant
constriction of the heart,
is ten times worse than
setting its body to ground
on this block where two guys
whip pennies at an old man who,
having dropped his groceries, tries
to collect the rolling-away oranges
while they laugh.

NEIGHBORLY GESTURES

Pollution in the hardware—
there's no escaping,
the low-hanging clouds spell
your name in wet-cotton cursive
and fill themselves
with sludge, with oil, with a mass
of slurry just waiting to release—
and here, we rush from storefront
to storefront trying to open a door
but no help arrives—in one, an old man
locks his palms to the handle
and sways back to block us out
and we are on the street open, naked,
unprepared for what is coming our way,
this pension of suffering
that is inevitable, but also so easily remedied
as that man disappears behind the blur
of his own breath, masking the glass.

THE ALTRUISTIC VANDAL,
DOING THIS FOR ALL OF US

It's a small investment to chip
away at the brick wall in this alley,
scraping a name no one will see,
where I dedicate this umbrella of sky
that watches, neutral,
no consciousness unto itself, just watching
as witness to know that here, just
as I thought I reached my limit,
I could keep going, shards of clay
falling to ground, releasing judgment
in the eye on the side of a building.

THE COST

We are in a room
in a building
with a thousand rooms.

There are no windows.
It is always light
but there are no lights
in the room.

The walls are white,
the furniture is white.
There are mirrors
on the wall
that reflect
the opposite wall
but do not reflect us.

Touching the glass,
we don't leave
imprints. Breathing
onto the glass,
there is no steam.

On the table
in the center,
two full glasses of water,
the glass so clear
it appears
as two cylinders
of water, held
by a manipulation
of gravity.

No shadows are cast
in the room.
No prisms of light
through the glass.

We speak endlessly,
but there is no sound
and trying to shout
feels like inhaling
without exhaling.

There is a single door,
noticeable only
by the thin margin
along its border,
revealing its heavy
concrete body.
No doorknob,
no keyhole,
no darkness
holding its edges.

At the door's side,
a steel box,
moss formed along
its corners, gray and white
galaxies of mold
on its surface,
and a circle opening
on its face,
sharp blade of a mouth.

You can leave
this room
but have to put
your hand inside—

the mouth closing,
cleaves it
in a clean sweep.

Pull your arm out,

raw bone and muscle
cauterized
and the door
angled open.

You can leave,
but it will be
like this.

And the ones who stay
are left alone
with nothing but
a severed hand
in a box, silently knowing

the moss and mold
will spread across
the white, white eyes
in the walls.

RIVER SIDE, RAIN SIDE, FIRE SIDE

A flare when you cough words, a disappearing act when you dance.
This rainstorm is from no cloud—the sun's exploded and sprays boiling water.
Yes, I am talking about you.
You whispered a secret into my ear, and I spoke a piece of paper.
I have built a tower designed to reverse lightning back to the sky.
Your eyelashes pull toward the moon.
Night's white pearl drowns the flames from your fingertips.
Danger isn't a bomb, danger is a drip.
I will build a thousand bridges, if that's what it takes.
The river is a tongue, and the tongue is of a holy beast.
Open, open your eyes, even if they have no iris.
Your hand in my hand, your mouth in my ear.
The rain won't stop, and it won't stop burning.

AT THIS VERY MOMENT

—the sun, perched behind the Eastern Building,
held up by electrical tape like a kindergarten
cardboard set for a play about the city.

We cough dust wind,
cloud for a magician's entrance,
a magician's exit.

In this moment, every single body on the street
turns to paper, each held to pavement
by a brick, fluttering in the rush of a pickup truck

that barrels through downtown, carrying
traffic cones that will turn to people
as pigeons pick away their plastic.

And in this very moment, our eyes earthbound,
the sun will crash to the ground,
neon wreath cutting into the buildings, coloring

the now dark sky—

2.

YOU WILL PRAY TO WHAT WE GIVE YOU

A golden blanket covers the city,
the neon and streetlamps finally busted open,
the power gone out along Grand Avenue,
so all that's left is the reflection
of a full moon in all that shattered glass
caught in smoke and fog like stars in gauze—

—and as we look above to the source,
that moon births a sun in front of our eyes
and we are blinded, with no choice
but to fall to our knees and praise the light
with all we have left, as it is all we have left.

THE ALMIGHTY IS A KLIEG LIGHT

This curve of sky, inner landscape of my eye—
the moon, pupil in reverse.

Your eyes are my eyes—
in my hand, your heart, a useless onion.

Stop staring at the necklace around my heart—
an abacus of threaded knuckles.

My fist made of a million knuckles—
I will knock a sermon out of you if it kills me.

Not hillside, but a stub-toe-sermon—
a crushed letter with kidnapper's lettering.

Hidden behind litter roadside,
every streetlamp in the world is one of my million eyes.

Step into the moon-negative—
I'll never find you—

no matter how many craters I make looking.

JULIETTE AT THE BUREAU

In a room where you remove your ears
like earrings and wipe your mouth clear
like lipstick, there are prayers in the walls
written by your alternate self, periodically
traversing the universes held together
by this antique bureau, its mirror scratched
from the inside by lightning and when you tell
a secret, she knows what you are going to say.
Kiss the envelope, leave it next to the lamp—
those lip prints will last the decades to the point
they become vintage and free of context-gravity.
And meanwhile, in another galaxy,
you weep openly into an empty jewelry case.

I'LL BE YOUR KEEPSAKE

I'm in the box, along with your thousand unstamped letters
and termites crawling over their ink.

Fingerprints lift themselves from my hand,
stretch out like a line of music, and away.

I told you it would all lead to this.

My chest, merely a cabinet for a mason jar holding
chalk conversation hearts smashed into a fine powder.

You wrote a poem on the back of a cabinet door
but I can't move to read it anymore.

Please, recite it by memory,
please. I want to remember its words,

even if I cannot move
to do so.

MEMOIR CAR

A car made of bones
ramshackles down the road,
its pistons the eyeteeth of
a rust-faced beast.

You left letters behind,
a suit, an empty bottle,
and a ring on a string
from the chandelier.

The road rises and falls behind,
as if water-logged pages
from a submerged book,
the first and last line the same:

save me.

THE TUNING FORK
AND THE LISTENERS

The reader has a condition,
tries to reconcile the tone
of words with melodies using
a tuning fork, a lovely sound
but a cheat to civilization-building
as we sing along too easily,
too ready to launch into a
chorus before deciphering the words,
no precision whatsoever, reciting
a Bible full of redactions and blurry text
in the basement while broadcasting
into a tin can tied to a tree trunk,
while your family has been locked
in a room upstairs, trying to shout,
but it is too late
as the crowd outside
rips off each other's arms,
singing a hymn by heart,
every second person limbless,
and the ones who are not,
damned to never know
what they have done.

MAGIC

I snapped my fingers and they caught on fire.

I winked at the sun and cried a diamond.

I touch your back, my hand turns to a bouquet.

The breath of a tree overhead
carries the sound of a thousand raindrops.

IN THE TREES, ON THE ROAD, OFF THE HIGHWAY

Firecracker in hand, matchbook
encased in the fist of my heart,
a burning car roadside and footprints
leaving soot in a Rorschach parade.

Wearing a blanket of leaves,
dark green folds over my shoulders,
I've carved your initials in a tree
with a thousand initials in the tree already.

The vanishing point of the road
ends in your open mouth, the pavement
the tonal concrete of your voice,
an endless song echoing past the forest.

A deer leaps in the woods, but in the trees,
far overhead, a great airborne animal
birthed when no one was watching, no one
but me, looking for you.

SPY AND DEPART

Standing on the roof, weather vane broken,
my spine, the lightning rod.
Birds nesting below in street-side garbage bins.

I'm flashing a light across the street
toward the house that's been empty for sixty days.
A single hand touches the cracked glass.

It's no business to identify that palm—
somewhere else on this street,
someone's doing the same to me.

I'm here to light the roof on fire, smoke
signals to the planes that weave above
this grid of bungalows.

May they take me from these espionage streets,
quickly back to the one I love.

MEET ME IN THE CITY,
LEAVE ME AT THE STATION

Climb in the cab with me,
the joints on the door wink
as we enter, then move
through the city, a river-set leaf.

In the lip of the backseat,
it is easier to disclose secrets,
it is easier to predict a response
and to wish it to the passing cars,
and when we reach our station,
spring arrives.

The station where you leave me,
the station with a train made of taxis,
where it all makes sense and
a newspaper with headlines
sun-bleached to ghost text
blows against my ankle as you leave.

THE AIRFIELD TRAFFIC PATTERN DIS-PLACEMENT CEREMONY

Light up the exhaust pipes,
the jet on the runway,
a thousand mosquitoes wait
to be blown off the surface
of an inconsequential city lake
only to return or regenerate.

In caves, candles lit by no one,
a ceremony has begun,
the ghosts of this park
raise a toast, moments here
that echo and turn
to ether inside rock.

The first kiss,
the run that ended in disaster,
the drugs done behind the soccer goal,
every song sung out of tune
now a melody of EKG lines etched
on a stalactite as if an ancient language

long past deciphering.

DISSIPATE AND OBFUSCATE

I am learning
to be alone,
I am learning
to let my limbs
float away, tethered
to my torso
by a leash, so that I
hover over the possibility
of this yard.

I am mist,
I obscure the observers,
and I circulate
my circulation
into the rhythm
of water, so that

no one can see, and
no one can find me, even
when I light
the stove on my return,

as I drink a cup of tea
and disappear in its steam—

HEART HOLDS LAKE

Lakeside, I crouch—
still enough
light before night, the reaching
branches reflect
to make a shimmer-wreath
around the water's border.

A mockingbird holds bark,
builds an altar, whether it realizes
that fact or not. A beetle works
its way between the chips.

I remove my left hand,
set it on the water,
watch it glide across the surface
until it is out of view.

Next, my right ear,
then feet, forearm,
ankle, rib cage . . .

Until all
that is left,
my heart in my open palm
along the water,
finding its way out,
seems to rise
like a torch of blood

then sinks
to the bottom of the lake.

TIME TRAVEL BARGAINING TACTICS

I summon you, Lord of Time,
by setting out the inner pieces of thirteen
watches across the backyard's picnic table,
making a body with their mechanics—
minute hand for nose, hour hand for mouth,
the circle shell of their bodies for eyes—

I swallow my pride, speak your name, just
loud enough to make it real, just loud enough
and you appear,
thrift-store suit, leather tan face, and wrinkles
sanded down across your forehead.

When you smile, it is clear
that one of your molars is a fang.

I ask you to stop time for me,
and your teeth make an umbrella
and the long-dead tree behind you
pushes out a green leaf.

We strike a deal: my right arm
to stop time, my left to reverse at will.
And I let you take them—
each limb in easy motion.

I look around. The leaf on the tree is actually
a moth, having crawled from behind a branch,
that spreads its wings in a struggle

then twitches then dies
and falls to the ground.

And when I look back across the table,
you swing my own arms like loose baseball bats,
beating me down and laughing, every gear,
every screw jumping up and down on the table.

When it stops, I open my eyes, find
you gone, the watches reassembled, and
on the ground, a thousand dead leaves,
and on the table, a single fang for a clock.

3.

HOMECOMING TIME BOMB

With a dead man's switchblade,
I carve my name into a concrete wall,

the wall the border to the city
of my birth and the city nothing
but skeletons and car shells.
Stray dogs feed on wild strawberries
grown from vines binding bodies.

The past doesn't go away, of course,
it just hides like a thorn-face
imaginary friend standing beside you
at all times, stuffed with a time bomb.

And, naturally, anyone who says
they regret nothing has never done
anything truly regrettable.

I'd lay the city bare if I could,
breathe in a match and exhale
flame, just quickly enough to settle into

the space between breaths on a clock.
Before the clock explodes.

GARGOYLE

In dusk's leather sheet, curtains
draw close and closer against a solar
explosion, an atom-burst song ringing
through the skyscraper sprawl, its
spine the corpse hand of a witch,
darkness sewn together by lightning,
the stich of thunderclaps like bodies
falling on the world's largest bass drum
while the towers' breathing gargoyles
grow impatient, their teeth rotting
from the inside out, their wings
turning to tissue paper, to cluttered wax
that will fail their flight on the first attempt
to snatch you up,
limping off midair with only a lock of hair—
an iron-seed tear drops not from empathy
but from the inability to rip you apart
when they had the chance.

YOU ARE A JELLYFISH, GHOST

The bridge, like an unhinged elbow,
spreads across the river.

Each car flees the city, and the paint on homes
appears to attempt escape, as well,
instead looking like loose fingernails
held on by paper-thin cuticle.

It is quaint to picture ghosts here, hovering
robed skeletons with threaded muscle
singing standards in reverse.

But go out tonight—
the fog spreads the light farther,
but thinner, and you see it—
a jellyfish, bioluminescent,

floating at your eye line,
its bulb the size of a skull,
a human heart inside its cup,
a lock of hair trailing beneath.

DISGUISED DOPPLEGÄNGER

Here, in this too-small sweater
of summer, I walk outside
to lean on the fence,
hope for wind.

There is wonder in the diamonds
of the chain-link fence,
a document of the days, each pocket
names the past, showing a prismed earlier
version of myself, costumed as a child,
only visible for a moment when
the sunlight lasers, then mazes, itself
off a nearby car's windshield.

And then it's gone. It's gone for good.

DEAR DEMON

You sent a demon to do the Devil's work,
but his eyes don't frighten me, the snake mouth
in his pupils when he stares.

The quick jump to startle me does nothing,
his teeth like ivory screws, the breath like
burning hair doused with arsenic—it's all
a little much and easy to laugh off.

If I may offer advice:

get up here yourself, but make no spectacle,
simply sneak behind me, tie sacks of concrete
flecked with flower petals to my ankles,

weigh me down in place, and then lean in—
whisper in my ear—*good, now walk away
or walk beside me.*

BOMB THE SUBTEXT

When the windows blew out,
the frame was a broken jaw,
busted lip bleeding into the house.

Shards of glass on the floor,
confetti for the taking, and our skin,
spotted with it, stinging, raw.

There are no secrets left,
everything is through a bullhorn
and the shadows bleached.

While we cower in the bathtub,
whisper a prayer for the unsaid,
for all our teeth set squarely

in our mouths.

MISDIRECTION MECHANISM ACTIVATED

Watch, watch, wait—
giant arachnids patrol the city
with a thousand eyes that run down their legs,
chase away the crowds on the street
while you lean down to pick up the handkerchief
of the greatest grifter in all the land,
a dollar-bill-patterned piece of satin,
while he whistles a song and the people are gone,
and you are left holding a tissue used to squash
a bug on the windshield of a police car which was
just about to hit the town, looking for you, or someone
like you, and there's nowhere left to go when everyone else
has claimed hiding spots, climbed into escape hatches,
bolted down their locks, and started eating each other's limbs
far before hunger has truly set in.

THE PARTY

1.

You received an invitation.
On the invitation, a blueprint of a building.
On the envelope an insignia of a clock-faced sun,
an arrow through its core.

2.

The building is on the outer rim of the city,
the street with the sinkhole from the last storm.
Above its entrance, a bas-relief of a god
assembling the world, or taking it apart in pieces.

3.

In the vestibule, a crate of old fruit,
strawberries now white with fur.
In the lobby, a blue doorman's hat, upside down,
a beetle scurrying along its insides.

4.

On the sixth floor, the top floor,
a block of sun cubes itself through the hallway.
The carpet pattern starts as two thick lines
that turn to lightning bolts further down.

5.

Near the window, the dead end of the hallway,
a one-armed bartender prepares your cocktail.

On his eye patch, mother of pearl circled
by stitching of a solar system.

6.

Speechless, he makes your drink:
water in a mason jar, then six spoonfuls of sugar,
then, from an eye dropper, six tear drops of arsenic,
then more sugar, a thin slice of horizontal lemon.

7.

A chair sits at the hallway window and you take it.
Behind you, the bartender walks away,
picks up the dropped orange, heads down the stairs.
It is silent.

8.

You clutch the armrests, a skull carved into each elbow.
Through the window, you see the sinkhole,
looking like the imprint of a missing boulder,
like the busted mouth of the Earth.

9.

Reaching for your drink, your arm
is a phantom limb.
Looking in the glass,
an iris cups the surface of the liquid.

10.

And you can see out the window:
a compass of bodies, from all directions,
walk toward the hole, wordless,
climb in and vanish.

11.

Never even breaking pace,
never hearing you shout
stop at the top of your lungs
through a mouthless face—

12.

—as they disappear, disappear,
disappear.

X-RAY DIAGNOSIS HYPOTHESIS

Imagine a spine with a vein
wrapped through its length,
a thin blue snake pumping blood
around bone. Imagine a heart in a liver,
pumping a bile pulse, and picture
a cage of ribs holding nothing more
than a loose globe of wet hair,
a twisting planet of nerveless ribbons.

You have eyes in your ears,
a merry-go-round of lungs
turning through your torso.

The IV drip's hanging arm asks,
Is this good, do you like this?
The monitor responds for you
in jagged red lines,
He is a jar, he is polluted, he is still.

And when a person enters, it's a doctor
in a lab coat draped over a tuxedo
who whispers a question to the window,
but your voice is a formaldehyde cylinder,
a four-legged fish crawling up glass.

THE FOG IS A FIRE,
THE FIRE IS A SIGNAL

From the top of one of the few remaining
skyscrapers, the rest of the city looks like
a mangled hand, fingers broken and skinned,
cracked bone never healed.

The morning fog gathers itself
into the caverns of downtown,
settles like cotton strung between
blown out, glass-jagged windows.

As the sun rises, for a moment
it lights the streets from below,
the hovering gauze turns
pink, then red, then white.

I want to scream down,
shout to people
I want to be there,
but aren't.

I am missing something
that isn't there. I am missing
something that was never
there to be hidden.

Nineteen crows circle
this building like a crown,
waiting for a clearing

to dive down, search for food.

At any moment, that fog will light
on fire, a rolling fist of flame,
burning letters off street signs,
handprints off glass-faced doorways.

And as the blaze tires itself out,
its gray breath rises, I am
in the heart of a smoke signal,
signaling . . .

I look down at the streets,
now clear and shadowless,
and see only you,
you,

looking up, never to see me waiting.

THE SKY DOESN'T WANT
YOUR MYTHOLOGY

Launch a vase of thorns into the sun,
watch those fangs burn to seeds
that bloom in red reverse on their return,
revisit the Earth as bloody rain,
our attempt at beauty futile
yet rising for a moment first
to convince us we are eternal,
only to fall, fall back with the stain
and blade of hidden motives,
leaving us raw, burning, marked
with the face of an angry star
we created in the first place.

THE SUN AND THE GROUND
CONSPIRE ETERNITY

The sun bakes the pavement
so it stays warm underneath, growing
the bioluminescent grasses downward
for the lawn of the underworld,
where we send our avatar bodies
on that negative landscape,
reenacting our performances
as movies that will run then burn out
like celluloid and ultimately—
if we're lucky—
feed the lawn as it grows
and grows again like hair
long after we're gone.

REPEAT AND AGAIN
REPEAT TOGETHER

Each moment of the day drops
straight from the sky as a sliver,
dropping in a vertical line,
lodging itself into our skin—

revealing the pure darkness that hid
behind the blue and cloudy mural above,
to leave thin, translucent spikes
sticking out from our arms, our legs.

And as the curtain above turns
to black with the absence of time,
we lie here, backs on grass,
dew climbing up and over our thighs.

If I remove your needles, will you
remove mine? Take your time—
we will pull each out, breathe on the spots
left behind, and put them in a satchel.

We will carry that bag every day—
and every day, gather up more,
and every day, wind up in darkness again.

ACKNOWLEDGMENTS

Thank you to the journals where the following poems initially appeared:

A Dozen Nothing: "The Almighty Is a Klieg Light," The Branch," "Bomb the Subtext," "I'll Be Your Keepsake," "Heart Holds Lake"

Blackbird: "River Side, Fire Side, Rain Side," "Time Travel Bargaining Tactics"

Forklift, OH: "At This Very Moment"

Gulf Coast: "You Can't Escape When You've Been Underwater All Along"

Gramma: "The Airfield Traffic Pattern Displacement Theory," "Welcome"

Inter/rupture: "Homecoming Time Bomb"

The Manhanttanville Review: "The Party"

Muse/A Journal: "Magic," "Now, Breathe Fire," "The Sky Doesn't Want Your Mythology"

Night Block: "One Attacks the Other," "Phantasmagoria at 6 AM"

The Normal School: "Neighborly Gestures," "Repeat and Again Repeat Together"

Packingtown Review: "Gargoyle," "You Are a Jellyfish, Ghost"

Passages North: "Divinity," "Juliette at the Bureau"

Superstition Review: "This All Starts With You, and This All Ends With You"

Watershed Review: "The Sun and the Ground Conspire Eternity," "You Will Pray to What We Give You"

Zocalo Public Square: "In the Trees, Off the Road, On the Highway"

Zone 3: "Spy and Depart"

Thank you to the people who helped with many of these poems:
Pete Miller, Trish Murphy, Sarah Pape, and Elizabyth Hiscox. Thank you to Mom, Dad, Keith, Emilie, Thomas and Eva. Also, thanks to the Bakers. Thanks to Pauline Uchmanowicz for her time and care with this book, and Codhill Press for their support.

Love and special thanks to Sarah Baker.

ROBERT KRUT is the author of *This Is the Ocean* (Bona Fide Books, 2013), which received the Melissa Lanitis Gregory Poetry Award, and *The Spider Sermons* (BlazeVox, 2009). His poetry has appeared widely, such as in *Blackbird, The Cimarron Review, Gulf Coast, Passages North,* and *Poetry Vinyl.* He lives in Los Angeles and teaches in the Writing Program and College of Creative Studies at University of California, Santa Barbara.